150

PROFESSIONAL

HORSERACING

SYSTEMS

150 PROFESSIONAL HORSERACING SYSTEMS

by the editors of
GAMBLER'S BOOK CLUB

GBC PRESS
P. O. Box 98115
Las Vegas, NV 89193
www.gamblersbookclub.com

GBC Press books are published by Gambler's Books Club in Las Vegas, Nevada. Since 1964, the legendary GBC has been the reigning authority on gambling publications and the only dedicated gambling bookstore anywhere.

Library of Congress Catalog Number: 2011925829
ISBN 10: 1-58042-280-2   ISBN 13: 978-1-58042-280-2
GBC Press is an imprint of Cardoza Publishing

GBC PRESS

c/o Cardoza Publishing
P.O. Box 98115, Las Vegas, NV 89193
Toll-Free Phone (800)522-1777
email: info@gamblersbookclub.com
www.gamblersbookclub.com

T TABLE OF CONTENTS

6. TWO-YEAR-OLD SYSTEMS 39

TABLE OF CONTENTS

7. SERIOUS HANDICAPPING SYSTEMS   53

10. INTERNATIONAL HANDICAPPING SYSTEMS   95

TABLE OF CONTENTS

.

1 INTRODUCTION

Our goal in this book is to make you a winner at the track! Inside these covers, you'll find the bone and sinew of 150 horse race selection systems currently used by many professional horse handicappers around the world. In more elaborate format, some of them sell for up to $100 each!

This new edition was completely edited and redesigned, and we've added charts, sidebars and more explanations throughout to give you more winning tools. Since 1964, the Gambler's Book Club in Las Vegas has been the reigning authority on gambling publications. Handicapping systems is one of our specialties and we're thrilled to bring back this classic in updated form.

This book was neither hastily nor thoughtlessly thrown together. Indeed, the original editors of this classic stated: "It is doubtful that any such compendium has received more care and more critical appraisal than the fast and simple, indeed bedrock, systems between these covers."

You have enough handicapping systems and ideas here to greatly refine or even change your approach at the track. In all, you're getting thousands of dollars in value for just a few bucks. We hope you enjoy this book and profit from its advice!

2 SYSTEM OBJECTIVES

The first task of any system is to cut the player's losses. This is of paramount concern. Then, by means of the system's effectiveness—coupled with the player's skill and supported by sound money management principles—the final test is a net profit at the end of the races.

Any system is better than thoughtlessly picking horses at random. Of this, you may be sure! And any system is better when you apply astute money management principles to its operation, so we've included some brief suggestions on monetary systems—plus some words of wisdom from experts at the thoroughbred game.

If you are a more serious player, we give you plenty of useful tips and systems to increase your bottom line. If you enjoy going to the track only now and then, you can have a lot of fun using one of the simpler systems we present. Some of these betting methods require only a peek at the daily racing page, while a few require nothing more elaborate than reading the track program.

We begin with general tips on handicapping. Follow them and you'll be closer to the money trail that ends at the pay window. To all you horse racing fans, good luck! And don't be bashful about making a small bet. A $2 winning ticket has given many a rich man a special thrill.

Words From the Wise

"Gambling is more than mere recreation. It is an essential fact of life. It derives from and faithfully expresses the uncertainties of the universe, as embodied in the laws of chance. These laws account in great measure for the shape and tone of our existence. As a creature of chance in a world of chance, man spends his years making choices and taking flyers. He gambles for bread, for love, for fame, for security, for survival. And sometimes he gambles for the fun of it."

—Tom Ainslie

3 HOW TO BECOME A WINNING BETTOR

Who doesn't want to become better at something? A better dad, better tennis player, better cook—and of course, a better handicapper. But how?

Let's start off with a how-not-to: If you are betting every race on the program, you are a losing player. Refrain from such behavior! Bet no more than two or three races on the daily card. The feature race of the day and events with larger purses will prove to be easier handicapping riddles than maiden races, dashes for two-year-olds and "spectaculars" that are complex to handicap in terms of distance, weight and form.

If you become confused or baffled at the track, try one of these remedies:

- Sit the race out.
- Buy a $2 ticket on the favorite and relax.
- Better yet, go home and wait to play another day.

The professional bettor is always prepared to lose as much as he'd like to win. This means three important things to you as an occasional bettor:

- Do not reduce the amount of your bet after a win.
- Don't double your bets after a loss.
- Always follow your predetermined plan.

Words From the Wise

"The winning horseplayer is not the man who holds the proper set of dogmatic beliefs, but the one who can observe and adapt to the ever-changing conditions of the sport."

—Andrew Beyer

Now, let's get on with some solid handicapping advice, the how-to of becoming a better bettor.

12 RULES OF WINNING

1. Avoid chitchatting with other race players. Anybody who knows anything worthwhile won't tell you anything.
2. Keep daily racing notes and make them brief. Short notes every day will serve you far better than a bunch of complicated figures that you work up now and then.
3. If you are good at observing the price lines, you'll find your best prospects in fields of six to eight horses.
4. If you like to play longshots, you'll do best with fields that have eleven or twelve horses.
5. Speed figures produce more winners than systems based only on class and class drops. Class plus weight-off add up to the most reliable figures of all.
6. Be selective not only with the horses you bet, but with the races you bet.
7. A horse that has previously started over today's race course is usually better than one that has yet to take a trip around.
8. A strong rider is better than a weak one. Many a jockey who can do 95 pounds can do nothing else.
9. There are people training horses who couldn't train a pig to eat! When you figure a race, make the trainer an important element in your handicapping.
10. It's 1,000 to 1 that any bad habits on the part of the horse were picked up from the bad habits of all the people who have worked with him.
11. Jockey streaks—winners and losers—tend to be longer than trainer streaks.
12. Ouch! If your horse keeps bobbing his head enroute to post, dipping his nose to right or left, save your money: He's sore in a foreleg. Bet this horse to lose.

THE BASIC QUESTION IN HANDICAPPING

In Greek mythology, Diogenes searched diligently for an honest man. Whether he ever found one is up for grabs! We handicappers seek an honest thoroughbred.

People tend to tell convenient lies and distort the truth to fit their goals. A horse never! His record tells his story for him—and it's always in plain sight in the *Daily Racing Form.* Search your soul—or better yet, the form—for the answers to these three questions:

- Is my horse running into form or losing form?
- Can he handle the competition today?
- Do his odds reflect an overlay on his chances to win?

That last one is the most important. To put it another way, "Am I getting an overlay if I bet on this horse at these odds?" That is the basic question in handicapping.

The handy collection of sound and workable handicapping systems we have carefully compiled in this book will do nothing to help you find integrity in your neighbor. But it will help put you in touch with truthful horses at honest prices!

Words From the Wise

"The supercharged, nervous and emotional tension apt to be generated in an individual visiting a race track to make bets renders him peculiarly vulnerable to impulses to do thus and which in fact may be inimical in the extreme to his chances for success."

—Robert S. Dowst

---

4 A SUPER SYSTEM

We begin our list with a simple system that has proven to be a thoroughbred itself. This chapter is short but sweet—it contains one of the best methods of play ever originated. Read it carefully, be sure you understand it perfectly, and then you can begin playing with confidence. You won't wear yourself out making trips to the pay window, but when one of these horses shows up, he runs like a banshee!

SYSTEM #1
SUPER SYSTEM

With this system you can make a flat or equal bet on each selection. The *Daily Racing Form* gives several sets of selections by various expert handicappers. Here's the key: When all these handicappers name the same horse as their first choice—or when one of these handicappers names a horse as his second choice and this same horse is named as first choice by all the other handicappers—make this horse your selection, provided he won his last three races.

This keeps you on the most consistent horses, those that are at the peak of their very best form. It is this added protection and play control that makes this little jewel the nearest approach to perfection ever attained in the field of horse racing systems.

Handicapping Time:
5 minutes reading the program

Words From the Wise

"It all depends, not upon the horse, but upon you. In my many, many years of experience in the racing world I have found the most difficult thing is to teach the public how to win; because the most essential quality is patience, and next to patience comes courage, and that is all very well, but occasionally you find that the courage has to come before the patience, and that, alas, is where so many hundreds, nay thousands, of members of the betting public fall by the wayside. They have the patience to wait and win, but they lack the courage to lose and then win, and so therefore, to avoid losing you must have the courage to lose, because by that you will subsequently win. The mentality of the multitudes of our betting public is like the mentality of a grasshopper, hopping here and hopping there, hopping from this place to that."

—Stable Scout, Leamington, England

5 PROGRESSION AND UNIT BETTING SYSTEMS

Everybody knows how it feels to pick five winners in an afternoon—and then go home tapped out. This collection of progressive, unit-betting systems will help you manage your money while still getting some kicks out of handicapping.

SYSTEM #2
EDNA'S SPECIAL

This one probably sounds like the daily special at your local diner. It isn't. It was one of Edna Luckman's (co-founder of the Gambler's Book Club) favorite plays.

Here's something to ponder: Three winners at 3-2 add up to the same reward as one winner at 9-2. In capital risked, however, the formula is $9 for $6 as compared to $9 for $2. The respective chances of winning vary depending on the number of entries in each race. For example, the contender in a six-horse race has 1 chance in 6 to win and must beat five horses. But if he is bet to place, he need beat only four horses.

Betting the horses is more a matter of getting money value than your percentage of winners.

Handicapping Time:
Only as long as it takes to read the program

SYSTEM #3
HORSE PARK CHOPS SYSTEM

Glitter Gulch Gus, denizen of the Las Vegas craps escarpments and former horsebook operative, plays the Chops system at dice. It's pretty simple, really: Bet up one unit when you win, and bet down one unit when you lose.

Converting this to a torrid scheme at horse parks, here's a money method that's great if you're running hot. If you're ice-cold, it at least provides 20 plays before blowout.

Starting with a $100 bankroll, place your wagers in $5 units. If you win, go up five units. If you lose, go down five units. Your stop loss is your total bank. If you hit some overlays or longshots, rent an armored Brinks pleasure vehicle!

Handicapping Time:
Only as long as it takes to read the program

SYSTEM #4
DOUBLE-X PROGRESSION

My uncle Dennis was a Double-X guy if there ever was one. He'd bet Show Me Your Stuff in almost every race the nag ran, rain or shine, win or lose.

If you like to bet one horse until it wins, increasing or doubling your wagers, try passing one or two races after he first runs out. For example, this might be your progression if you pass his second race, that is you cross it off or "X" it out: $2 on his first run; X his next race; bet $4 on his third run; progress to $8 and then to $20.

The true Double-X progression would look like this: $2-X-X-$8-$20.

If your "stable" horse (the one you wish you had in your dream stable) wins 20 percent of his lifetime starts, for instance, your percentage of catching his winning race is 60 percent (three bets in five starts).

You have avoided the normal doubling-up progression that would read $2-$4-$8-$16-$32 with an investment of $62 while covering with only $30. If your horse should win the second or third time, you're out only $2. In fact, you can pyramid several horses with a reasonable outlay using the Double-X system of play.

Warning: Progressions are *never* recommended for 2-year-olds, maidens, or fillies and mares.

Handicapping Time:
Only as long as it takes to read the program

SYSTEM #5
SUPER CHALK

Way back in the days before electronic gizmos took over so many menial tasks, the day's totals were posted on a chalkboard, yesterday's version of today's totalizator. As the betting neared post time, the chalkman simply erased the old odds and posted the latest totals. When a horse's odds kept getting better and better, it became the "super chalk," a term that has lasted long since chalk went out of vogue.

When you bet a super chalk horse—the strong favorite—remember that when the crowd bets all horses in a race, the average loss per set of odds on the board (9-5, 7-2, 5-1, 6-1, 15-1, and so on) should figure out at 18 percent (the pari-mutuel takeout). However, favorites win one-third of the races on average, and show a loss of only about 9 percent. This occurs because players still go for the longshots despite the fact that their losing percentage on their longshot picks can be substantial.

In other words, the average favorite is an overlay. This means that the super chalk will pay more to win than his actual chances are to win. Therefore, it makes super sense to separate the strong favorites from the run-of-the-mill public choices. Just use whatever system works best for you.

Bet these super chalk horses to win or place according to what the pari-mutuel prices indicate. At the point where you outdistance the crowd's pick by 18 percent, you'll make money. And that's a super result!

Handicapping Time:
Only as long as it takes to read the program

Words From the Wise

When a major error in handicapping the chances of a horse is to occur, make certain that this error is on the part of the crowd—not yourself. When the crowd lands heavily on a single horse to win, find a logical way or combination of ways to bet against that horse. When the public is seeking to "raid" the entries by stabbing this way and that for its choice, select a solid horse—and go with him. Move unilaterally against the public.

—George Herman

SYSTEM #6
THE BIG CIGAR

Don't blow smoke at this system until you've tried it. If it works for you, you'll be smoking fat stogies with the big boys!

Play the first four choices to win, betting at the ratio of $4 on the first choice, $3 on the second, $2 on the third and $1 on the fourth. Make flat bets only. This system works best on large fields and open races.

Anybody for a Havana?

Handicapping Time:
Only as long as it takes to read the program

SYSTEM #7
WIN TARGET FORMULA

Although the development of money management techniques based on a percentage of your bankroll has evolved into a nearly foolproof science, many race fans still prefer the older win target method of betting.

With this system, you first choose the amount of money you want to win for the day. Let's call it your profit target. Then you divide that by the odds showing on the totalizator board. It's the simplified way of determining each individual bet size.

Here are some examples of how a win target formula works.

WIN TARGET FORMULA			
Profit Target	Odds	Math	Wager
$30	3-1	30 ÷ 3 =	$10
$30	5-1	30 ÷ 5 =	$ 6
$30	15-1	30 ÷ 15 =	$ 2

When you hit your total target profit for the day, go home! You're through taking risks, you've won the game, and tomorrow you can go for an encore.

Using this win target formula, you'll run into two basic problems. First, after a losing race or races, you must add your net loss to your desired daily profit and divide the odds into that figure to reach the amount of your appropriate wager. Further, if you bet win and place using this plan, allow four times as much capital to back your play.

Handicapping Time:
Only as long as it takes to read the program

SYSTEM #8
BALANCING THE BOOKS

Let's say you're at the track and a race comes up where the favorite is either odds-on or is very short-priced at 4-5, for example. Further, a field of two, three or four horse is entered as a single betting entry, sometimes called a coupled entry. How should you bet the race?

In races like this, where the favorite is odds-on or is very short-priced and two or more horses are entered as a coupled entry, you may find it favorable to wager on two, three, four or even five horses to win. Be sure to adjust your betting units in accordance with the odds shown on the tote board.

Let's hope you'll be able to balance the books with the bottom line showing a profit.

Handicapping Time:
3 minutes at the track.

SYSTEM #9
DUTCHING AGAINST THE FAVORITE

When you dutch a race, you bet on several horses in the exact ratios that are required to make an overall profit. That way, no matter which horse wins, you win. In other words, you can net money on all your wagers. An enticing idea, isn't it?

Here is a formula for dutching a race against a strong favorite. This simple chart shows you the exact amount to bet according to the odds of each horse in the race you decide to dutch. For example, if your first pick is going off at odds of 3-1, bet two units on him to win; and if your next pick is 5-1 to win, bet three units on him to win.

DUTCHING AGAINST THE FAVORITE	
ODDS	WAGER
3-1	2 units to win
5-1	3 units to win
5-1	2 units to place
7-1	3 units to place

Handicapping Time:
3 minutes at the track

SYSTEM #10
THE BERRIES

Looking for chalk horses fit and ready to win? Try using the George Berries system. When two or three "figure horses" go postward, handicap the race down to a fly's eyelash. Back the potential winner at an overlay price reward.

If several strong contenders are in the race, pass—it's a guessing game. If just one solid play is entered, pass—the price will be an underlay.

Use your present method of selection, which should include a high-percentage, short-price system. Place win bets only. The price will be okay because of the division of public support on this flight.

Handicapping Time:
Only as long as it takes to read the program

SYSTEM #11
S. O. S. AT 6 TO 1

This is an unusual system developed by Eddie of Las Vegas, a sharp player who plays the "puzzle horse" at 6 to 1. Should he be 3-1 or 10-1? No telling! The puzzler isn't out of it—and he's not in. He's no bum and he could pop up. They don't have 61 slumps, you know!

Bet any horse at 6-1—on the schnozzle only.

Handicapping Time:

Only as long as it takes to read the program

SYSTEM #12
WAGERING SCALE

This simple progressive wagering system is based on a betting scale. Using it, you place wagers in sequential amounts of 2 units, 4 units, 6, 8, 10, 12, and so on, according to your pick's winning at certain odds.

Here's the wagering scale to follow:

WAGERING SCALE	
ODDS	**RETURN**
1-1	1 point
7-5	2 points
9-5	3 points
2-1	4 points
11-5	5 points
12-5	6 points
13-5	7 points
14-5	8 points

If you want something easier, make your bets one degree back after a win at 1 to 1 or less, two degrees at better than 1 to 1, and three degrees at 3 to 1 or better.

Follow the selections of any good handicapper. This one's a winner!

Handicapping Time:

Only as long as it takes to read the program

SYSTEM #13
BET-DOWNS

Play the third choice to place *if* he gets backed down two points in the tote action. For example, suppose Super Saver is the third choice in the eighth at Santa Anita. He was posted at 8-1 and then got backed down to 6-1. Or maybe he started at 5-1 and got backed down to 7-2.

Put a place-bet on him and hopes Super Saver runs a super race.

Handicapping Time:
5 minutes at the track

SYSTEM #14
WELL-MEANT MONEY

In following well-supported horses—those with odds of 5-2 and less—use the following unit betting scale:
1, 1, 2, 2, 3, 3, 4, 4, 5, 5, 7, 7, 10, 10, 15, 15, 20, 20

Some bettors use the same moderate progression for casino games where good runs are frequent.

Handicapping Time:
Only as long as it takes to read the program

SYSTEM #15
THE SECOND SLOT

This system revolves around a scale of wagering at pari-mutuel prices that will show a profit—if. The "if" part means that you can make a profit if you use a public handicapper's selections and play them to place only.

Here's the scale:

1-2-4-6-10-14-21-28-41-54-74-94

Handicapping Time:

Only as long as it takes to read the program

SYSTEM #16
CRAFTY

They say this wagering scale is a humdinger! We don't know who "they" are, or exactly what a humdinger is, but whatever floats your boat, they say.

Let's say your original bet size is $2, which we'll refer to as "x." After the first event, you bet 2x, win or lose. For example, if you wager $2 on your first bet, the 2x would make your second bet $4. The 4x would make it $8, 6x is $12, 10x is $20, 16x is $32. Test it, using any good handicapper's selections.

The scale is:

2-4-6-10-16

Progress up one whether you win or lose. On breaking the scale, start over. It may look goofy but check it out for a few days. With a crafty handicapper, they say it works great!

Handicapping Time:

Only as long as it takes to read the program

SYSTEM #17
SLOT MACHINE

Here's a nifty system that promises all cherries, no lemons! Play sprint races that are not more than 6 ½ furlongs. Play to win on the two horses carrying the highest weights. Then add the bets you placed on the first race to each successive losing race until you make a profit. Bet the same amount on each of the two horses.

It's like getting a two-line winner on any decent slot machine!

Handicapping Time:
2 minutes at the track

SYSTEM #18
WORLD SERIES SYSTEM

This wagering system involves a series of wagers, something like the tournaments in the World Series of Poker, which have progressively bigger buy-ins. Follow any good handicapper's selections with this betting method.

Start your first series (Series 1) with a $1 wager. If that loses, wager $2 on the next race. If that loses, bet $3 on the next. Should that also lose, start Series 2 with wagers that progress 2-4-6. If all three of these lose, start Series 3, which would be 4-6-8, and then on to Series 4 (6-8-10).

On winning, deduct the amount you've won from your losing wagers, starting at the last losing wager.

Believe it or not, one winner in three at odds of 3-2 will show a profit!

Handicapping Time:
Only as long as it takes to read the program

SYSTEM #19
LISA'S POST PLAN

Here's a lollapalooza from Lisa, who likes laying bets only at post time.

In five-horse races, play one unit on the post-time favorite to win. Play two units on the post-time second choice to place.

Handicapping Time:
Only as long as it takes to read the program

SYSTEM #20
8-5 TO 4-5 BRACKET

This dandy little system owes no man a dollar! Play only those favorites that range in price from 4 to 5 up to 8 to 5.

Is that all there is to it, you ask. Yep!

Handicapping Time:
3 minutes at the track

SYSTEM #21
SHORT PRICE REAL NICE

Want some interesting statistics?

Favorites closing at odds of 7-5 or less on the totalizator win 46 percent of their races and place 68 percent of the time. Odds-on favorites closing at odds of 3-5 and less win 68 percent of their races and place 86 percent of the time.

What's so interesting about these stats? They dramatize the importance of watching for overlays in the *place* slot. They also point to the safety of making progressive wagers on odds-on horses to place.

Handicapping Time:
Only as long as it takes to read the program

SYSTEM #22
THE LOOSEY GOOSEY

It's longshot time! And that means open range on loose-goose odds hiding in the shadows of the tote board. In races where the top three favorites show loose-goose odds—5-2, 3-1, 7-2—longshots can be lurking at 8-1 and up.

This type of pari-mutuel action is marked by "fluttering odds." That is, the odds fluctuate as one and then another horse shows up as a weak favorite on the tote board.

Find the longshot and hope he shoots out of the shoot for a wire-to-wire win!

Handicapping Time:
5 minutes at the track

SYSTEM #23
FAST, SURE 'N EASY

Who doesn't want a sure and easy system for winning? This one comes your way when two horses that are owned by the same person are paired as a single betting unit in the same race. They're often called a "coupled entry" or simply an "entry."

When two horses of a coupled entry are *both* selected in the consensus at 1-2 or 1-3, and both go postward, you've got a place-bet special at your fingertips. Easy, huh?

Handicapping Time:
10 minutes at the track

SYSTEM #24
WORLD BEATER

Perry from Pasadena, who never misses a meet at Santa Anita, calls this one a world beater. Take 4-5 on your money. If you can't get it on the favorite to show, then get it to place. If not there, then get it to show or place on the second choice.

Pass odds-on races. Also pass races where two equal choices conflict. You're not handicapping the horses, you're shopping for prices. It works for Perry!

Handicapping Time:
As long as it takes at the track

SYSTEM #25
W-P-S ODDS SCALE

You're in a quandary: "Should I bet Magellan in the sixth to win, place or show?" You just can't decide.

This scale should get you out of your dilemma and off to the window with ticket in hand.

ODDS SCALE		
WIN	Can bet if odds are:	2-1 or more
PLACE	Can bet if odds are:	3-1 or more
SHOW	Can bet if odds are:	8-1 or more

The odds are good that you'll like this one!

Handicapping Time:
10 minutes at the track

SYSTEM #26
50-PERCENTERS

Horses that finish in the money (first, second or third place) 50 percent of the time are good win-plays when they go to the post at odds of 5-2 and more.

If they go at 3-2 or less, they are promising plays to place.

Handicapping Time:
2 minutes at the track

SYSTEM #27
CERTIFIED PLAY

It's unknown who exactly "certified" this play, but it's a verifiable winner among a lot of bettors.

Play odds-on favorites to win *only* if the second choice is 4-1 or more on the odds board. Be sure you note the numbers on the odds board, *not* the figures on the morning line.

Handicapping Time:
As long as it takes at the track

SYSTEM #28
SHOW TIME

This is a "Bill, the Las Vegas Low Roller" special!

If only one of today's horses got in the money his last time out, he's a prime show play in today's race.

Handicapping Time:
2 minutes at the track

SYSTEM #29
POINT, COUNTERPOINT

This one is actually a plus-minus point assignment system. To come to a conclusion about which horse(s) to bet, you assign points for the in-the-money performances of every horse in the race. Count their most recent three races only.

Give each horse points according to this chart:

FINISH POINTS	
FINISH	POINTS
WIN	35
PLACE	25
SHOW	15
FOURTH	10

Total the number of points for each horse's last three races. Then deduct the total from the weight to be carried by the horse. The horse with the *lowest* point score is your play. For example, look at this chart:

Weight	Last 3 Races	Points	Final Figure
118	4-1-3	60	58

Handicapping Time:
1.5 hours with the program

6 TWO-YEAR-OLD SYSTEMS

Two-year-olds can be racing's most difficult division to handicap. Each baby in the barn is a potential star, so it takes some honest work and a few races to tell who's who.

Here are some dynamite systems for finding baby winners.

STRAIGHT ARROW

A two-year-old is the "square" of the racetrack. There's no tampering with him! He's straight arrow, running on good oats and clean hay.

Some two-year-olds don't reach full flower until they start racing as three-year-olds. At most, two-year-olds are going around no turn or one turn early in their career. These are straight speed dashes, first cousin to the quarterhorse sprints and the real live monkey-on-the-back greyhound pup races of years gone by.

If you're looking for some real action, bet the second-high weight to win if the favorite hasn't yet packed today's weight. Bet the second-low weight to show.

Handicapping Time:
1.5 minutes at the track

SYSTEM #31
GOOD RACE + WORK

Select a two-year-old that ran second in his last outing and showed fast subsequent work. Follow him three times, progressing by units in this manner: 1-2-5.

Drop the progression when he wins. And drop him if he fails to win during the three plays.

Handicapping Time:

30 seconds at the track

SYSTEM #32
TOTE A GOOD GUIDE

You don't even have to break a sweat with this dandy little system. When a two-year-old dash is carded as the third or fourth race on the program, let the tote board do your handicapping.

After the morning line gets its first revision with the opening betting flash, mark your program with the prices on every horse. Any horse that shows a 2-unit drop in the first flash odds by the time it is circling in front of the gate merits attention. For example, if the horse has dropped from 5-1 down to 3-1, 3-1 to 2-1, 2-1 to 8-5, and so on, focus on him.

If the higher-priced horse—5-1, for example—shows a sharper drop than the short-priced favorite, he's your play to win. If the favorite shows the sharpest betting action, he's your play to place.

What if no sharp odds drop? In that case, pass the race. Why? Because the backstretch is having problems separating them.

ODDS DROPS		
	1st Blink	Near-Close Blink
Favorite	7-2	5-2
Other Horse	4-1	2-1*
Favorite	5-2	6-5**
Other Horse	5-1	3-1
Favorite	3-2	1-1x
Other Horse	4-1	3-1x
Symbols Key		
*Your play to win **Your play to place x No play		

Handicapping Time:

5 minutes at the track

SYSTEM #33
BABY FAT

Baby Fat is a good system for betting the two-year-olds but it's for claiming stock only—absolutely no stakes or allowance races, or invitational events.

Play a first-ever winner to repeat until he picks up five pounds or more. Then shift to the second public choice or consensus choice. Double your wagering unit and bet the second choice to place if he's in at six pounds lighter than the runback horse. Otherwise, pass the race.

Claiming kiddies are uncertain propositions when taking on additional poundage. Higher-class juveniles, however, are chunky, studdish types that can pump the iron. Hence they do not fit this method.

Handicapping Time:

1.5 minutes at the track

SYSTEM #34
FORM VS. BLOODLINES

Maiden two-year-olds that have shown a touch of good form on the racetrack have an edge over expensive sire and dam bloodlines in fall and winter. In spring and early summer, bloodlines count more heavily.

"The time of year is a factor," Hall of Fame trainer Woody Stephens says. "If he is well-bred and his workouts are good, he could be any kind. If the race is in the fall, two-year-olds that have had a chance to run a few times and gain experience are often preferable to first-time starters, even those with an edge in pedigree."

Does this mean different figures for baby racers—a set for spring and a set for fall? Yes!

Handicapping Time:
One minute reading the program

SYSTEM #35
THIRD-TIME CHARMER

We've all heard that old expression, "The third time is a charm." It's often used by two-time losers at golf, slot machines and marriage! If you believe it, try this third-time charmer of a system.

If a maiden two-year-old colt is making his third start, and his best speed rating is within five points of the heavily-bet favorite, bet on him to win and place when the odds are 8-1 and rosier.

We hope you'll get a charming result!

Handicapping Time:
One minute reading the program

SYSTEM #36
GETTING THE SPEED

Let's get into high gear with this sharp system for two-year-olds competing in high grade claiming races during the first three months of the winter season, January through March only, and in races of two and three furlongs only. This system will give you a plentiful supply of "rated" horses.

Assign points to the entries in this manner:

- 5 points for each winning race to date
- 3 points for second
- 3 points if it went to post at less than 5-1 (but don't count races in which it was the favorite)
- 10 points for each handicap or stakes race in which it finished among the first half of all those entered
- 5 points if it finished in the second tier

If the colt wins two races, it gets 5 points for the first win and 2 points for the second win. If the colt runs two bad races in a row, discard your ratings card and pass him until he returns to form, starting from zero points. First-time starters get no points unless they are bet down to favorite. In that case, pass the race.

These point totals will give you ratings sizzlers for the opening 90 days of the year. Just hope they're not too hot to handle!

Handicapping Time:
Five minutes at the track

SYSTEM #37
2-YEAR-OLD PLATERS

The term "plater" used to refer only to the occupation of farriers, but over the years it has acquired two additional meanings. First, when a seasoned handicapper says a horse is a plater, he means that it isn't up to snuff—it hasn't shown much of anything in its past performances, so he considers it an inferior entry. And since platers are often entered in claiming races, the term also refers to a claiming horse.

Claiming races for two-year-olds place a premium on good gate boys, and that's what this system is all about. Keep a jockey chart for two-year-old claiming races. Log total mounts, wins, places, and shows. Then give points to each jockey based on the following percentages of his finishes:

JOCKEY POINTS	
In-the-Money %	Points
50%	7
40%	6
35%	5
30%	4
25%	3
20%	2
15%	1

Look back over your figures and add a simple + to any rider who has racked up a win or two. If he's been in the money for more than 50 percent of his, give him a score of 50 percent plus. If he's had three or more rides with no mounts in-the-money, deduct seven points.

If the rider is a new arrival at this track, use his stats for meetings at other tracks. Note that new arrivals seldom get mounts on the baby racers, except for nominated stakes events.

Your handicapping figures will be more in line—and will vastly improve in consistency—if you consider these rider point schedules before deciding to bet or pass.

Handicapping Time:
30 minutes at the track

SYSTEM #38
GOOD SPOT

In two-year old stake races, play the horse with the *least* weight. But wait—there's more to this system.

In addition to carrying the least weight, he must have previously run within 2/5 a second of the best time made by any horse in the race over the same distance as the present race. And, oh yes, he must be getting at least five pounds from the favorite.

Handicapping Time:
2 minutes at the track

SYSTEM #39
TOP RIDERS

Horses for courses—and riders for horses. And different strokes for different folks, especially when it comes to rating jockeys.

Remember this little gem of knowledge: The leading rider at the meeting is often the leading feature-race jockey. Okay, you know that already. But the leading jockey is seldom the highest-ranked rider in a two-year-old race. What does this mean for you, the bettor?

Bet jocks who have a winning record riding two-year-olds.

Handicapping Time:
5 minutes at the track

> ### Words From The Wise
> A good jockey, a good horse, a good bet.
> A poor jockey, a good horse, a moderate bet
> A good horse, a moderate jockey, a moderate bet.
>
> —"Pittsburg Phil"

SYSTEM #40
SLOW AT GATE

"A horse, a horse. My kingdom for a horse!" shouted the dismounted Richard III as the enemy was bearing down on him. I recall saying the same thing more than a few times at Hollywood Park!

If it's a 2-year-old winning horse you're looking for, check the program for one that got away from the gate in his last race among the last half of the pack and won by something other than a nose. That is, he won by a neck, a half-length, or more.

This baby figures to run beyond speed mark in this heat, even if it's been upped in class a bit. Betting three-furlong races and beyond is okay, but maiden races don't work with this at-the-gate and at-the-wire improvement system.

Handicapping Time:
2 minutes at the track.

SYSTEM #41
SPEEDY WAY

Maybe we should've called this one the S.O.S. method. Why? Because it's a simple and speedy way to handicap the 2-year-olds. Here's all you have to do:

Win-bet the top weights that came third or fourth in their last race. What if more than two mounts qualify? In that case, skip the contest—it's just too close to call.

Handicapping Time:
1.5 minutes at the track

SYSTEM #42
BABY PAYOFFS

Some of racing's biggest pari-mutuel payoffs happen in 2-year-olds racing between the dates of September 1 and December 31. These horses are racing only in their own age division and they aren't required to pack high imposts. ("Impost" is horse language for the weight that a horse carries.) Further, an abundance of talent and breeding-farm politics forces the tracks to card the races.

Here's a system that can lead to boxcar mutuels:

7 POINTS FOR MUTUELS

1. Throw out females carrying more than 116 pounds, even if all of them in the race are carrying that much poundage or more.
2. Eliminate the horses that were beaten by nine lengths or more in their last outing.
3. Eliminate maidens that are competing against winners.
4. Give any horse preference if he draws a light weight assignment.
5. Give preference to horses that have won $8,500 or more in purses.
6. An apprentice rider is acceptable if he has a record of at least three wins with the babies during 30 days.
7. Don't let a short-priced public favorite scare you off!

The kind of horse produced by this betting system is fully qualified to run well against highly touted "name stable" entries that can go off at short prices despite lackluster records.

Handicapping Time:
5 minutes at the track

SYSTEM #43
JAN'S JOLT

Who is Jan? She's the handicapper who developed this neat way to score 2-year-olds at prices.

Find the colt that was a non-favorite in its next-to-last race and either won, placed or showed—but in its last outing, the baby failed to get any part of the money. This sweetie may be a sleeper that goes all the way today at a price.

Handicapping Time:
2 minutes at the track

SYSTEM #44
TROUBLES COLUMN

Nobody knows the trouble I've seen—so goes the old song lyric. But when it comes to horses, you can easily find the troubles they've seen by reading the "Horses In Trouble" column on the track program.

If the program lists a juvenile colt or filly that has had difficulty at the gate—and if he was the first, second or third favorite in that race—it's a win shot today.

Handicapping Time:
5 minutes at the track

SYSTEM #45
THE LONE RANGER

This system calls for playing baby races only. First, search the program at the track like Tonto looking for clues to find the bad guys.

If you find that only one horse (the Lone Ranger, get it?) was either $500 higher in claiming price than any other horse in his last race—or if all of the last races of the horses entered were maiden races, and only one such horse either won that last race or finished second by not worse than a neck—that horse is your play to win his next time out.

Do not play muddy or heavy tracks, and make flat bets only. If you follow these guidelines consistently, you will find this one to be a winning system.

Handicapping Time:
5 minutes at the track

SYSTEM #46
BLINKERS

Use your blinkers to find a 2-year-old that has run no more than three races. If he finished within three lengths of the leader in his last outing and gets blinkers in today's race, he's good for a win bet if his odds are 4-1 or juicier.

Handicapping Time:
1.5 minutes at the track

SYSTEM #47
INSIDE, OUTSIDE

Suppose you discover a 2-year-old that's the favorite (8-5 or less), and he draws the rail position for the first time in his career in a five-furlong or longer race. Bet the *second* choice to place, regardless of any high, early speed the horse may have shown to date.

You also can bet a horse to show in the race if he's going off at odds that are in the 8-1 through 12-1 bracket *and* he's starting from the 10, 11 or 12 post position.

Handicapping Time:
3 minutes at the track

SYSTEM # 48
DEUCES & TREYS

You've discovered that New Horizon, a heavily-supported 2-year-old, has lost twice as the favorite. Still, he is not competing as a claimer.

Bet this colt to win in his next three starts, regardless of the odds. Use this unit progression with your wagers: 1 unit, 3 units, and then 5 units. If New Horizon wins any of his next three outs, stop the progression.

Handicapping Time:
Only as long as it takes at the track

Words From the Wise

The crowd at Aqueduct bet down seven consecutive losing favorites. The question is: Were the horses off-form or the people off-form?

—Huey Mahl

SYSTEM # 49
RUNBACKS

When a 2-year-old colt wins by two lengths or more, and runs back within 11 days, bet him to win if he has the same rider.

Handicapping Time:
30 seconds at the track

SYSTEM #50
GOING, GOING, GONE

Let's say you want to tab a filly to beat the colts in the fifth race, but only at a price. That is, you like the filly and you're looking for a good bet. Now suppose the track is muddy, she's been out more times than the male contenders, and she is getting a proper weight discount.

Under these circumstances, you can bet on her to turn the trick in the mud.

Handicapping Time:
30 seconds at the track

SYSTEM #51
SERIOUS YOUNGSTER

You're at the track and notice that a 2-year-old named King's Ransom is entered in the feature race, the event with the highest purse on the afternoon program. This colt is carrying 106 pounds or less, and he comes from a "name" stable that usually sends high-weight performers into competition.

Coupled with a star jockey up, bet this pick to defeat consensus horses, regardless of the odds and the competition.

You might even win a king's ransom betting on this serious youngster!

Handicapping Time:
5 minutes at the track

SYSTEM #52
THE NORTH WAY

After a 2-year-old colt has been claimed at $7,500 or more, pass his next two races. Then bet him to win, regardless of the odds.

In this "north way" system, fillies do not qualify. You might say the young ladies are the "south way," as many are claimed as future broodmare prospects.

Handicapping Time:

Only as long as it takes at the track

7 SERIOUS HANDICAPPING SYSTEMS

This set of systems gives you a slew of sharp and effective betting methods designed to keep pace with today's racing tempo. Let's start by listing the power factors you should consider in making profitable picks.

SYSTEM #53
POWER FACTORS

How do topnotch handicappers select their picks? Very carefully! They select which ponies to bet by thoroughly analyzing the following ten important factors to come up with solid betting choices.

> ### 10 POWER FACTORS FOR
> ### PICKING WINNERS
>
> 1. Is the top class of the race
> 2. Has the top speed
> 3. Must be in favorable form
> 4. Shows a sharp, short blowout (workout)
> 5. Was a going-away winner of his last race or was a torrid stretch closer
> 6. Shows a top rider aboard or a favorable rider switch
> 7. Comes from a sharp barn
> 8. Picks up no added weight and preferably gets a weight break
> 9. Has raced at least once over today's course
> 10. Has raced within the past 14 days

The best chalk systems derive from these power factors. The varying combinations of these criteria produce different systems of play. Sticking precisely to these 10 power factors listed will give you a master system that you can follow with confidence.

Handicapping Time:
1 hour reading the program

SYSTEM #54
SHIPPER'S SPECIAL

Seeking a winner for one of those cheap, homebred contests? That is, races for California-bred horses only, Illinois-breds, Washington State-breds, and so on. Just pick the colt or filly that has been shipped home from out-of-state.

The theory is that the horse will be so glad to be back at home he'll race his heart out.

Handicapping Time:
2 minutes reading the program

SYSTEM #55
ABC PREFERRED PLAY

Try this alphabetic play in classic races—that is, a race of 1¼ miles—or in races for cheap claiming platers.

In a series of races, let's say that "A" beats "B" in their first time out. Then "B" beats "A" when they meet for the second time. But in their third meeting, "A" beats "B" again, giving him a two out of three record over "B."

When you come across this set of circumstances, "A" will almost invariably beat "B" the fourth time.

Handicapping Time:
5 minutes at the track

SYSTEM #56
SOPHOMORE MAIDENS

Maiden route races can be excellent plays during the first four months of the year when the conditions specify 3-year-olds and up. A 4-year-old maiden can't be much of a horse, so a fairly sharp 3-year-old can handle the older stumblebum.

Look for the sophomore who is getting an eight or more pounds weight break. That puts him within striking distance—at a good price, of course.

Handicapping Time:
2 minutes at the track

SYSTEM #57
FINISHES & TOTAL HORSES

This solid system goes back six decades or more. It steers you not only to fit horses, but places a point value on the number of competitors a horse has defeated, an important factor that bettors usually overlook. Use the last three races the horse has run. Add its total finishing positions and divide that figure into the total number of entries in the horse's last three outings.

Here's an example that shows you how the system works. Bonnie Connie ran third, first and second in her last three starts while meeting fields of eight, nine and ten. The math looks like this: 3 + 1 + 2 = 6. When you divide 6 into 8 + 9 + 10 (27) you get 4, with a remainder of 3. Your rating would be 4, with a remainder of 3 or 4 to 3.

Eliminate horses that haven't started at least three times. They must have been on the track no less than 17 days back. A horse can pick up weight, but no more than 5 pounds additional. If the horse sheds one or more pounds, give it a +.

The horse with the highest points is your pick. This is a gilt-edged approach if you take the time to make your calculations.

Handicapping Time:
55 minutes reading the program.

SYSTEM #58
MIDWEST FIT HORSE

Midwest handicappers launched this one. It catches really fit contenders that are stretching out into longer races. Find the horse that won its last race within the past 25 days at today's track and is going a notch farther this trip.

Suppose Henry II won his last race at the same track as today, he's the choice at 5-2 or better, and is carrying the same weight or less. His last race was ¾ of a mile, and today he's running one mile.

Keep in mind that today's distance must be longer than the distance at which the horse won its last race. Here is the distance progression to look for:

DISTANCE PROGRESSION	
Last Race Distance	Distance Today
3/4 mile	1 mile (but not 7 furlongs)
7/8 mile	Pass the race
1 mile	1 mile 70 yards
1 mile 70 yards	1-1/16 or 1-1/8
1-1/16	1-1/8 (No play if over 1-1/8 mile)

If more than one horse qualifies, or if a female is running against the boys, pass the race.

Handicapping Time:
30 minutes reading the program

SYSTEM #59
RACEBACKS

This one requires a bit of record keeping, but it could prove well worth the effort.

Keep a notebook of all favorites that lost their first time out. Play these horses to win and place in their next start, provided they are back within 10 days—and no other horse is entered under similar conditions.

Handicapping Time:
5 minutes at the track

SYSTEM #60
FEATURE FAVOR

Racetracks big and small feature at least one race daily, and two or three on Saturdays and holidays. Feature races always lure the most consistent runners. The percentage of winning favorites in featured races at many tracks exceeds the normal 33.30 percent mark.

Here's your mission: Spot an outstanding race with an outstanding horse. Bet your pick to win and place. Just be sure that you know which tracks are yielding high percentages of feature favorites.

Handicapping Time:

5 minutes reading the program

Words From the Wise

In horse racing, the positive expectancy involves all the foolish wagers made by a public that's ill-informed. Your negative expectancy is the pari-mutuel takeout of 14 to 19%, or 1 in every 6 dollars that are gobbled up by the state and the track. In betting, you are making your own 'price line' in opposition to the crowd, whose line shows on the totalizator board. When your horse racing line is 20% or better than the public's and your money management is realistic, you win.

—Bob Baskett

SYSTEM #61
KANSAS CITY BOOKIE

We don't know which Kansas City bookie came up with this dandy play, but he's probably sorry he passed it along to his clientele since it's proven successful for so many of his customers.

Look for a horse that ran second and was beaten by two lengths or less carrying 114 pounds or less. Find a race in which this horse gets off five, six or seven pounds in weight from the time it finished second. Play these horses straight (that is, to win) and place.

To make this system more effective, wait until such a horse has run one race after you make him a system horse. Play all of your system horses twice if they don't win first out. Then drop them after they score.

Handicapping Time:
10 minutes reading the program

SYSTEM #62
CLASS

Here's a tiny tidbit of information that could make more than a tad of difference in your next handicapping venture.

Note the class of the race that a horse is entered in today. Is the horse entered in the same class as his last time out? Is he running in a lower class that last time? A higher class?

Depending on class of the race a horse is entered in today, horses run in the same or lower class than the previous race 92 percent of the time. They only run in a higher class than their last out 8 percent of the time. Take these stats into consideration in handicapping the race.

Handicapping Time:
Only as long as it takes at the track

SYSTEM #63
STARTER HANDICAPS

Here's out next tidbit of info to help you handicap a race. To sort out the field in a starter handicap, a horse's average purse earnings are the best clues to its class.

Handicapping Time:
Only as long at it takes at the track

SYSTEM #64
MALE VERSUS FEMALE

This one may sound sexist, but the statistics have no bias whatsoever. Excluding 2-year-old races, when mixed sexes compete against each other the males—colts, geldings and complete horses—win 75 percent of the time. Females—fillies and mares—only win 25 percent of the time.

These figures pretty well prove the point that the male is superior to the female when it comes to speed and strength. However, these statistics must be weighted to take into account the fact that females don't compete against the stronger sex all that often; hence, the numbers carry a built-in distortion.

Also, a stable hungry enough to match a female against male competition isn't always one of the sharper outfits, so the lassies aren't necessarily in able hands.

Handicapping Time:
Only as long as it takes to read the program

SYSTEM #65
FIXING SICK SYSTEM

Got a "sick" chalk horse system? It used to be good but now it's ailing? Try this remedy. Reduce your play to the one race a day that offers the highest purse. The race can have no more than eight starters. Wager one unit to win and three units to place.

The Systems Doctor gave us this prescription. He designed it to cure what ails you. He guarantees that your winning percentage *will* increase.

Handicapping Time:
30 seconds reading the program

SYSTEM #66
RX

"I got the horse, but not the prescription," handicappers sometimes say about claimed horses. Hence, this RX system for claimed steeds.

Give a claimed horse two outings before you consider betting on it. Bet the horse if it goes down in class from the claiming price—but only if it gets 5 pounds or more off and has a leading rider up. Play the horse for three races and then drop it. And if it wins at any time during the three races, drop it.

Handicapping Time:
2 minutes reading the program

SYSTEM #67
THE OVERLOOKED HORSE

Don't you just hate it when you overlook some important detail in a race and fail to bet what seems to have been an obvious winner—in hindsight, of course? Here's a way to gain some foresight and lose those hindsight blues.

Look for two horses—no more and no less, mind you—that have raced within the past 14 days. Both must have finished out of the money and both must have been beaten by no more than 2 ½ lengths their last time out.

If both of them are competing on the program today—and if the price on *both* horses is 7-2 or more—pick the one carrying the highest weight and bet him on the schnozzle.

Handicapping Time:
2 minutes at the track

SYSTEM #68
BIG FOOT

Don't confuse this one with the myth about some gargantuan creature wandering around in the woods waiting to pounce on its prey. This system's no myth, though it does refer to big-footed equines.

Big, strong horses have big feet. Bet the biggies to grab the money in the mud. Price is no object.

Handicapping Time:
Only as long as it takes to read the program

SYSTEM #69
CLASS IN CLAIMERS

If you like to handicap claiming races, you need a good system for evaluating the entries. Here's one that will help guide you in your choices.

In grading horses competing in the claiming ranks, the lowest price a horse has been entered for in the past 18 months outranks his highest price on a scale of about 4 to 3—unless the horse *won* at the higher price.

Handicapping Time:
40 minutes reading the program

SYSTEM #70
1-2-4 AND STOP

What happened to the "3" in this one? Hang on for a minute and you'll find out.

Find horses that gain five lengths in the stretch to finish second or third and not over two lengths behind the winner. When they are entered the next time out within 1/8 a mile of the same distance—and not over 3 pounds more weight under the same track conditions—play them to win.

If your pick loses, follow him two more times, increasing your bets in a ratio of 1-2-4. Stop when your horse wins.

Handicapping Time:
3 minutes at the track.

SYSTEM #71
AMY'S CHOICE

Watch the top choices of "Trackman" in the *Daily Racing Form*. When his top choice is quoted at 5-1 or more in the Probable Odds column and a different horse is named in the same race by another handicapper as his Best Bet, play "Trackman's" top choice to win. Or better yet, bet his pick to win, place and show in a unit ratio of 1-3-5.

"Trackman" is closer to the track action and comes up with ready performers who are tight as a drum and eager to win at nice prices. You can take his picks to the pay window!

Handicapping Time:
2 minutes reading the program

SYSTEM #72
GETTING PRICE IN MUD

Here's a good system for you longshot fanatics.

Bet the longest-priced pony in every race where the favorite is odds-on. This play works best in the mud. Bet your longshot on the schnozzle only.

Handicapping Time:
Only 30 seconds at the track

SYSTEM #73
PRIVATE PLAY

This has been referred to as the "Private Handicapper's Method." It is super chalk.

Take the consensus best bet from the *Daily Racing Form* for each track listed. If the horse ran first or second in his last race—and if he was also the favorite in that race—he is a standout play to show.

As a rule, this horse will represent the more formful competition—that is, truest to his past performance—on the afternoon menu, often going postward in fields of eight and less.

Handicapping Time:
2 minutes at the track

SYSTEM #74
FIVE BY FIVE

An Eastern horseplayer who calls himself George D. Winner inherited this "system" from an old buddy he used to play the ponies with. George swears that he shows a slight profit and never gets seriously hurt betting $5 to win on the fifth horse in the fifth race.

What's actually happening, of course, is that he's on a solid contender in one of the formful races on the program, and he's using a steady betting pattern that can easily withstand the losers until those "fivers" start hitting.

We'll give George the high five for coming up with this one.

Handicapping Time:
30 seconds at the track

SYSTEM #75
CHICAGO REPEATER

This Chicago special is worth repeating, so here goes. Winners repeat when, in their winning race, they beat the favorite by 1½ lengths or more *and* the favorite ran second to the winner. The horse must be running his next race over a distance no more than 1/16th of a mile from his win race and at the same level of competition. He also be carrying the same rider this journey with no equipment changes.

That Chicago action loves repetitious races! Let's hope you repeat their success.

Handicapping Time:
5 minutes reading the program

SYSTEM #76
TWICE HALTERED

First let's clear up what "haltered" means in horseracing circles. A haltered horse is one that has been claimed.

Now let's suppose that a twice-claimed horse in other than filly and mare races has been returned by the halter route to its first owner within 30 days of its last claim. Using the twice-haltered system, bet this horse to win in its second race *after* the second claim.

Handicapping Time:
5 minutes reading the program

SYSTEM #77
NEXT DAY PLAY

Look for a horse that has been scratched and then entered again the next day. Be sure the claiming price is not over $1,000 more for today, and today's weight is 3 pounds or more over the previous last race. This steed is what we call a "next day play."

Play all such horses to win, place and show in a unit ratio of $1 to win, $4 to place, and $6 to show. Add your losing race wagers to each successive losing race until you show a profit.

Handicapping Time:
3 minutes at the track

SYSTEM #78
GOOD THING GONE

Betting the favorite to show in the final race on the card is seldom an overlay anymore. That good thing is gone—just too many moneymen with wallets open and ready.

You're better off trying the second half of an exacta race, or the first half of the daily double. Even these pickings are rather slim, as faster tote readouts and sophisticated ticket vending equipment work against you here.

Handicapping Time:
Only as long as it takes at the track

SYSTEM #79
7-DAY RUNBACK

Trainers try to cash a purse when a horse is at its sharpest. Using this system, look for a sharp horse using these criteria:

- Any horse that held or gained in the stretch his last time out
- The horse is back in seven days or less
- A horse that is competing at the same or a slightly higher class
- A horse that does not add impost

When your pick has all these attributes, he is a solid shot today. Play to win only.

Handicapping Time:
10 minutes reading the program

SYSTEM #80
GETAWAY HORSE

Here's a system for claiming mares and geldings that are four years old and up.

Your getaway pick must have made its last start at a different track where it was well-bet (5-1 or less) and finished in the money. Today's race must fall within the "getaway" week; that is, the last five days of the meeting. The distance and weight should be right, and the horse's odds not longer than 6-1 and showing at least one point lower than the track program's morning line.

Your getaway horse should be a running horse out of a serious stable. Bet the front end only.

Handicapping Time:
3 minutes at the track

SYSTEM #81
THIRD TIME CHARMER

Looking for one of the best and simplest systems in existence? Here it is!

After a horse has run two consecutive races in the money without winning, play him to win in his next outing. If two of these horses are entered in the same race, play the one carrying the most weight.

Handicapping Time:
2 minutes at the track

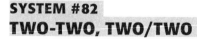

SYSTEM #82
TWO-TWO, TWO/TWO

The magic of twos works in this situation—good things, horses included, do come in pairs! This is our version of it.

Bet the horse that was second at the stretch call and second at the finish in his most recent heat—not more than (you guessed it!) 22 days back.

Handicapping Time:
Only one minute at the race

SYSTEM #83
MAKE-UP TRY

A jockey who was aced out of a race in which he rode a short-priced favorite and lost is one mad jock! He's looking to make up for his disgrace with a stellar performance his next time up.

That's the attitude that makes him a good progression bet for the next five races. Use these increments for your bets: $2, $6, $8, $12, $20. Stop when the jockey wins or when he runs out the string all tied up in knots.

Handicapping Time:
Only one minute at the track

Words From the Wise

Patience is the most important factor in handicapping. You get the chicken by hatching the egg, not smashing it. By sitting on it, not by cracking it.

—Arnold Glasgow

SYSTEM #84
SPOTLIGHT

Want a spot-play angle that could pay off big? Choose the event with the fewest entries and make it your own personal "feature" race of the day.

Here's our reasoning for the spotlight play: Say that five horses are coming out of the barn to meet a strong horse. They're mostly running for second, third and fourth moneys. If two or more races on the card tie for fewest starters, take the race with the highest purse and play your best horse there.

Handicapping Time:
Only as long as it takes to read the program

SYSTEM #85
HEATING UP

The cheap horse is at a low point when the atmosphere is sultry or a storm is brewing. When the weather turns hot and humidity drops, low-class horses often improve performance. Take a class horse in murky weather.

Handicapping Time:
Only as long as it takes at the track

SYSTEM #86
ADDING FINISHES

If you like to play longshots only, look for a race where one, but not more than two, horses finished in his last five races not farther back than fourth, and he did not win his last race.

If you find two such horses, add the finishing positions of their last five races. The one with the highest total is your play to win. If they tied on their totals, take one that finished the farthest back in his last race. Tied again? Pass.

Long prices make flat bets okay, but playing only longshots results in longer runs of losers than any other system of play. Buyer beware!

Handicapping Time:
30 minutes reading the program

SYSTEM #87
95 OF 100

When a coupled entry of two or more horses is the favorite and both horses are regarded as having a strong chance of winning, you can make a profit by making place and show bets.

Just be aware that books refuse large show wagers on this play because approximately 95 out of 100 entries of this type actually do show.

Handicapping Time:
Only as long as it takes to read the program

SYSTEM #88
SUPER CONSENSUS

Develop your own custom consensus by taking only the "Sweep" and "Trackman" picks from the *Daily Racing Form*. Add one other source factor: the selections of the most consistent daily newspaper handicapper in your area.

Enter their top three choices on index cards. Score 5 for first place choices, 2 for second choices, and 1 for third (no best bets). The maximum point total for any horse would be 15. The least total for a mentioned horse would be 1—in other words, you'll come up with a spread of 1 through 15.

Then check the tote board odds. Where the odds are an overlay—that is, more than the percentage of the super consensus point total indicates as proper—you've found your horse!

Handicapping Time:
1.5 hours reading the program

SYSTEM #89
ALLOWANCE WINNERS

Sometimes the racing secretary allows horses a reduction in the weight they carry, thus the races they run are called "allowance races." A horse may get a break in weight if he's a three-year-old racing against older steeds, or if she's a female horse racing against males.

My racing friend Stanley vows that allowance races are events where the racing secretary's friends have licenses to steal. " He can set up conditions favorable to any stable on shed row," Stanley argues.

Maybe yes, maybe no, but either way, allowance-class horses post good win percentages. You just have to know how to bet 'em.

In this very simple but sound system, determine whether today's favorite was also the favorite in the last race he ran and won, provided that test was also for allowance horses. Disqualify the horse if it picks up more than two pounds.

Handicapping Time:
2 minutes reading the program

SYSTEM #90
BOOKMAKER'S HEARTBREAK

When the handicappers who make the experts' selections in the *Daily Racing Form* agree on the first three finishers in a race—with the exception of one horse—that horse is the "dirty shirt" of the race.

The horse that receives a *single* mention among the selections—whether to win, place or show—often has been picked by a handicapper who knows something the others do not.

When this horse wins, it's box-car figures at the pay window!

Handicapping Time:
1 minute reading the program

SYSTEM #91
7-RACE RATINGS

Rate the last five, six or seven races of each horse in past performances *if* all of them have had as many as seven races. Give each horse 5 points for each win race; 4 points for each time finished he finished second; 3 points each time he finished third; 2 points each for fourth; and 2 points for each fifth-place finish. Now, total the points.

The horse with the highest total is your selection. In the case of a tie, take the horse named nearest to the top in past performances.

Use this betting progression: 1-1-1-2-2-2-3-3-4-4-5-6-7-8-10. If you show no profit at the close of this scale, repeat the scale, using double your initial wagers. Stop at any point that you show a profit. Make all your bets to win or all your bets to place, whichever you prefer.

Handicapping Time:
1 hour reading the program

SYSTEM #92
SOMEONE WAS ELECTED

Something like a political election where one candidate among the contenders has to win, one horse has to be the consensus horse in every race at the track. In a flipflop race where the consensus keeps changing, a real cheapie can score with the handicappers.

Look for a horse with a 25 percent win rate and a 33 percent in-the-money consistency factor before supporting one of the weaker consensus chargers.

Handicapping Time:

10 minutes reading the program

8

SPEED HANDICAPPING SYSTEMS

Good speed marks are excellent handicapping tools. These won't keep you up all night chewing your fingernails or overloading your computer trying to come up with winners. Only a few of these dandy speed systems takes more than an hour, and most require only a few minutes of your time after you reach the comforts of the track.

SYSTEM #93
SPEED MEASURE

You can put fast and fresh speed efficiency ratings on horses by developing your own numbers. You can use your numbers right out of the can, so to speak, or you can compare them with the *Daily Racing Form* numbers to spot standouts.

Here's a simple method you can use with confidence. Divide the winner's time by the time your horse recorded in his last race. For example, if the winner's was 1:11.2 and your horse's time was 1:12.4, simply divide 1:11.2 by 1:12.4 and you get .989, which is your horse's speed rating. Count 2/5th, 3/5th and so on as .2 or .3 when punching these figures into your calculator.

This SR (speed rating) system tells you how any horse did against what the competition did in the horse's last race— rather than some mythical speed mark derived from a horse's time versus the track record. It is especially valuable in placing speed numbers on veteran campaigners that tend to "do what they have to do" to win the contest. In other words, they are racing against horses, not track records.

With this SR system, any horse that won its last race receives a perfect 100. Now, when handicapping the winners of their most recent races, divide their running time by the best time in which each individual horse has ever run the distance. This is how you come up with his speed efficiency factor.

You'll spot scorching speed with this system. Just hope your pick does the same!

Handicapping Time:

1.5 hours reading the program

SYSTEM #94
KICKOR

Fainthearted sprint horses that steal an early lead in the slop often hold their speed better than they do on a fast strip. This happens because, in terms of flying slop, they are the "kickor," not the "kickee."

The time to bet this type of horse is when both the favorite and the second-choice horses are stretch runners. Many "bad weather" pari-mutuel bonanzas come from this precise racing situation in 5, 5 ½, 6 furlong, and one-mile races.

Handicapping Time:

5 minutes reading the program

SYSTEM #95
CLOCK WATCHER

This one is a clock-watcher's dream system. Most seriously contested horse races are events where de-acceleration sets the pace. That is, the pace is speedy at the start with a steady slowdown after 3/8 to 1/2 mile all the way to the finish wire.

Be on the lookout for horses that can do these three things:

- Show an early turn of speed
- Take back for a breather
- Come on again for a quick final quarter

Most of these types of horses compete in the highest caliber of handicaps and allowance races, but every now and then a plater will display this kind of talent. And guess what? He'll win when heavy money is down! Just hope you spot him before post time.

Handicapping Time:
10 minutes reading the program

SYSTEM #96
CONTESTED EARLY SPEED

Here's a nugget of knowledge you'll want to remember forever and ever: If there are two or three very fast horses in a race, one or two of them will quit before getting to the finish line.

Find a good jockey—one who will rate (save) his horse in a carefully-paced effort throughout the race—and put your money on him.

This system came down through the ages from George E. Smith, aka Pittsburgh Phil. And he got it from a long line of sharp horsemen before him.

Handicapping Time:
30 minutes reading the program

SYSTEM #97
SPRINT HORSE IN ROUTE

Here's our next knowledge nugget for your consumption.

The first effort of a sharp sprint horse going a route is usually a conditioning for distance. His second effort is for all the marbles.

Handicapping Time:

5 minutes reading the program

SYSTEM #98
SCRAMBLERS

No, we're not talking about scrambling a Denver omelet. Here's what we have on the menu:

When two high-weighted speed horses start from post positions 1 and 2, or from 1 and 3, they can get off to ragged starts with jamming along the rail if one gets away off-balance or develops any other difficulty when the barrier swings open. These ragged starts occur during the run to the first turn.

The degree of potential impedance is for each individual handicapper to assess, but it is certain that light-weighted speed ponies will break faster, cleaner and sharper than they will when shouldering big burdens. So, look for speedsters carrying the lighter weights in the race.

Handicapping Time:

Only as long as it takes to read the program

SYSTEM #99
THE NUMBERS GAME

Sharp selections can come from the old "numbering" method. Give 3 points for first, 2 for second and 1 for third in each horse's best-finish race during the past 120 days.

If any horse finished winner or second by a nose or a head in the last 21 days, eliminate him from consideration. The horse with highest point total gets the nod.

Handicapping Time:
1 hour reading the program

SYSTEM #100
BASE SPEED FIGURES

A simple calculator comes in handy for this system. Total all the speed ratings of the horses entered, using each horse's speed ratings for its most recent two races. Divide the SR figure by the number of horses in the race. This is your basic figure.

Then recheck the horse with the highest speed rating in his last race. If he has a total of five points more than one half of your basic figure, bet him to win.

Handicapping Time:
55 minutes reading the program

SYSTEM #101
ON THE BIT

Watch for horses that led all the way and then won drawing out; that is, they won going away from the field.

When these horses win by four or more lengths at odds of 4 to 1 or better, play them to win, place and show the next time they win. Use a ratio of $2 to win, $4 to place and $8 to show.

If they take on over five pounds above their win race, or are entered at more than a $500-higher claim price than the win race, either pass or bet the horse to show only. Add first bets to each successive losing race until you show a profit.

Handicapping Time:
10 minutes reading the program

SYSTEM #102
FLASHED, FADED

Suppose Mighty Malone flashed early speed in his last try over this same track, and then faded. If MM drops 10 percent to 15 percent in class, he packs suitable weight, and he comes from a hustling stable, you are justified in placing an across-the-board bet on him.

Otherwise, fade out of the betting picture—or you may be broke in a flash!

Handicapping Time:
3 minutes at the track

SYSTEM #103
FAST QUARTERS

Search out the horse with the best average of opening and closing quarters at 6 furlongs in his last start. He's a solid selection to win today.

Just be sure to disregard this speedster's middle quarters, as you're only interested in his first and last quarters using this system.

Handicapping Time:
1.5 hours reading the program

SYSTEM #104
COLT .45

You'll have a good shot at making a profit if you aim to find a lightly-raced colt with these requirements:

- Finished not worse than 4th at 5 furlongs or more in his last out
- Drops slightly in class today
- Has the same or better jockey on top

• Ran his last race within 21 days and/or had sharp drill no more than five days back

Shoot over to the pay window and hope he hits the target for you!

Handicapping Time:
3 minutes at the track

SYSTEM #105
3 WORKOUTS = 1 RACE

In this system, you consider a horse that has had three workouts during the past 10 days as having run one "race" in that period of time. If his workouts qualify as being swift times, check to see whether this horse qualifies under the terms of your present system of play.

If he does, do not pass go, go straight to the betting window!

Handicapping Time:
10 minutes reading the program

SYSTEM #106
TIME BOMBS

This systems works on the premise that, like a time bomb that's been set to go off at midnight rather than at noon, beaten favorites can come to life in a later race.

If the favorite ran fourth as the public choice, then posted a sizzling workout, and came back to race again within 10 days, he's your pick.

Just hope he blows the competition out of the water today, not next week!

Handicapping Time:
Only as long as it takes to read the program

SYSTEM #107
CONSISTENT & BACK

You can comfortably bet a consistent horse that didn't win his last time out, but has been a reliable racer and is back in the saddle again.

Bet this horse to win if:

- He's two or more points best in speed ratings
- He's back in action within eight days or less
- He's consistently been in the money 50 percent of the time over the past six months
- He finished no worse than third in his last out, but did not win

Handicapping Time:
5 minutes at the track

SYSTEM #108
SPEED + 100'S

Let's say you're considering betting Firefly in the fifth, but you're not sure what performance rating to give him. Try this "Speed + 100's" method in placing your bet.

Add Firefly's highest speed rating within the past 27 days to 100's in class. Subtract the odds from his last outing from his speed rating. From this, subtract the total of the last three calls on Firefly's last race to get his adjusted performance figure. (Note: This formula calls for a $5,000 purse to be rated as a "50" or as 50 100's.)

Handicapping Time:
40 minutes reading the program

SYSTEM #109
HANDICAPPING 7 FURLONGS

Now, horse fans, take a look at this simple but effective solution to the 7-furlong, speed-handicapping dilemma in which you sometimes find yourself.

Check the entry board for horses that have won at 7 furlongs in the past. If only one horse qualifies—and if he's competing against the same class of horse he's beaten at *any* distance this year—bet one unit on him to win and three units to show.

Yessirree, you have a livewire on your hands!

Handicapping Time:
1 minutes reading the program

SYSTEM #110
SPEED MARKS AFTER LAYOFFS

How do you put a speed rating on a horse that hasn't raced recently? You could play eeny-meeny-miney-mo, but we have a better system for you.

You can take the horse's best form and deduct 10 points from that figure. And/or you can make a speed mark by checking out his morning workouts. Driving is the fastest workout, so just take 5 points off his racing time. Handily would mean about 10 points off his racing time, and breezing would be 15 points off.

If your horse worked five panels in 1:02b (breezing), or 72 on a mythical speed chart, you'd add 15 for the breezing and establish an 87 for him. Then, subtracting 10 for the layoff, he'd draw a 77 rating.

Handicapping in these situations is a matter not only of knowledge, but also feel—that is, giving it the master's touch. Heck, even famous paintings must be touched up now and then. The results you get depend on your feel for it!

Handicapping Time:
10 minutes reading the program

9   WEIGHT HANDICAPPING SYSTEMS

Just about everybody wants to lose weight, and hardly anyone ever wants to gain it. The same thing goes in the equine world. We may not be able to advise you about your weight situation, but when it comes to the ponies, we have plenty of systems to help you figure out the significance of weight in making your picks.

SYSTEM #111
HITTING HIGH-WEIGHT ACE

Here's a handicap race selection method for feature events with purses of $50,000 or more. In handicap races, the racing secretary or the track handicapper adjusts the weight of each entry in order to equalize the field of contestants, similar to a golfer's handicap.

This betting system is designed to take advantage of the racing secretary's seemingly extreme reluctance to hand out high weights to star horses while giving bloated weight concessions to fill the race with cheaper horses.

There are a lot of "ifs" in the next sentence, but bear with me!

If the handicap race is 1-1/16 mile or longer, if the top-weight horse is the favorite, if he is carrying at least three pounds more than the second choice, and if he has not previously won with this impost, bet the second choice to win—but only if the second-choice horse has won by one length or more in the past and was carrying the same or higher weight against the same or better horses.

What if the second-choice horse in the betting doesn't qualify under these rules? In that case, turn to the other end of the scale. Starting with the lightest-weighted horse and proceeding up the list through all the horses that are getting a 12-pound break or more in the weights, find the lowest-weighted horse that has won in the past with at least five pounds more than the weight he is carrying today. Bet him to show.

These rules do *not* apply to any race that is one mile or under.

Handicapping Time:
5 minutes at the track

SYSTEM #112
THE HI-LO

Check out the weights the horses are carrying in all of the races on today's card. Consider only the horse carrying the *most* weight and the horse carrying the *third-lowest* weight. However, if more than one horse is slated to carry the same weight as the third lowest horse, pass.

Check every race, marking the most-weight horse and the third-lowest weight horse for each race. Your picks will be the one horse in each race that is carrying the *third-lowest* weight and is showing the greatest difference in weight with the top horse in that race.

Bet your pick to win and show. Or you can bet across the board, depending on the type of wager you prefer to make. You also may play one or two selections if you want to.

Handicapping Time:
1.5 hours reading the program

SYSTEM #113
HANDICAP WEIGHT FORMULA

This peach of a system is for handicap races only. In surveying all the horses in a race when you're handicapping a field, take the weight each horse is carrying seriously.

Here's how the formula works: Start by considering each pound a horse carries as one-fourth of a point. Suppose Fleet Frankie earned a speed rating of 92 in his last race while carrying 108 pounds, but he's carrying 120 pounds today. Calculate the difference between his two imposts (120 minus 108) and you'll get 12. Multiply the 12 pounds difference by one-fourth (.25)—you come up with 3—and subtract 3 from 92 and voila!

In this race, Fleet Frankie gets a handicap speed rating of 89.

This system will separate the peaches from the pits!

Handicapping Time:
5 minutes at the track

SYSTEM #114
TOP, BOTTOM WEIGHTS

Here's a method of selection based on the weight-carried factor. Follow these three simple rules and this system will work wonders for you savvy bettors.

In 2-year-old or maiden claiming races of 5½ furlongs or less, select the horse carrying the heaviest weight. In races over 5½ furlongs, choose the one with the lightest weight.

In claiming races for any and all ages that are 6 furlongs or less, select the horse carrying the heaviest weight. If the race is over 6 furlongs, select the one with the lightest weight.

In all handicap, stake and derby races that are any distance up to 1 1/8 mile, select the horse carrying the heaviest weight.

If the distance is over 1 1/8 mile, take the one with the second or third lightest weight, choosing the horse with the most purse earnings this year.

Handicapping Time:
1 hour reading the program

SYSTEM #115
WEIGHT/ODDS COMBO

Like a fine wine, this old-timer merits your attention. In the race of your choice, deduct each horse's morning line odds from the weight he's carrying. The high figure is your play.

Take a look at this example:

WEIGHTS/ODDS COMBO			
Horse	Weight	Morning Line	Weight/Odds Combo
Vegas John	117	2-1	115
Nuncio Type	116	12-1	104
Bobby Boy	122	3-1	119

Your play is Bobby Boy. This vintage system has scored many a winner for observant fans!

Handicapping Time:
5 minutes at the track

SYSTEM #116
WEIGHT

When you're handicapping the entries in a race, keep these statistics in the back of your mind. They'll help you sort the wheat from the chaff.

Horses run approximately in this manner in relation to the weight they're carrying in today's weight:

WEIGHT STATISTICS	
Weight Change	**Percentages**
Same as last race	47%
More than last race	22%
Less than last race	31%

Handicapping Time:

Only as long as it takes to read the program

SYSTEM #111
NOT LATE AT GATE

Have you ever tried pushing a wheelbarrow loaded with bricks? You had a hard time getting off to a good start but once you did, you moved right along, right? Now you know why high weight on a horse can cause him more trouble at the start than at the finish when he's highballing it down the lane.

This phenomenon is remarkably true of green juveniles when they're asked to carry other than their "scale weight;" that is, the weight they're accustomed to carrying in official weight-for-age races.

Tab a horse that is getting a weight break and bet him to beat a heavily-weighted favorite. But wait! Don't bet him if the favorite has won in the past when carrying the same poundage he carries today.

Handicapping Time:

Only as long as it takes to read the program

SYSTEM #118
CLOCKWORK

This method works like the proverbial Timex watch that keeps on ticking without taking a licking. When any horse that is 3-years-old and up is assigned a weight that he has not yet carried to a win before, avoid him if that weight is more than 121 pounds.

If a horse with these attributes is favored in the wagering or in the daily handicapping selections, bet the second-favorite to place.

Handicapping Time:
At the track 2 minutes.

SYSTEM #119
GRADED WEIGHTS

This one takes a tad more time than most of our other systems. But you'll consider it time well spent when you're standing at the pay window with your winning ticket in hand!

Use only the last four races of each horse. First, add the number of lengths the horse was beaten in his last four races. For example, if horse was beaten by 2, 4, 3 and 1 length in his last four races, the total would be 10. Write down this figure. Next, add the total weight carried by the horse in his last four races. Divide this total by 4, which will give you the horse's average weight carried.

Then see what weight the horse is carrying today. If it's less than his average for the last four races, subtract 1 point for each pound.

Here's how it works:

If the horse's average impost is 110, and he's in today's race with 106, *subtract* 4 points from his handicap figure. Or, if the horse is carrying 115 pounds, *add* 5 points to his handicap figure. Consider one point *either up or down* for each pound above or below the average weight the horse carried in his last four races. This is important, so be sure to make this allowance.

The horse with the *lowest* figure is your pick. Play him to win, place and show.

Handicapping Time:
2.5 hours reading the program

SYSTEM #120
TURKEY SHOOT

You don't have to limit this method to Thanksgiving Day at the races. You can use it any time you want a system that works with both sprints and distance journeys.

First, eliminate horses that are carrying 112 pounds or less. Then eliminate those with imposts of 120 pounds and more. If one of the mounts you eliminated is the favorite, play the second choice in the race to place, regardless of weight. Got that?

Handicapping Time:
10 minutes reading the program

SYSTEM #121
WEIGHT OFF IN MUD

When a mud race field of 12 horses and all four "also-eligibles" have failed to finish in the money in the past, bet the two horses carrying the lowest weights to win—if they have shown a mud marker in their past performances. Totally disregard their odds and their jockey.

Handicapping Time:
5 minutes reading the program

SYSTEM #122
WEIGHT AT GATE

Races for fillies and mares are difficult to handicap. Human females, chauvinists say, are impossible to figure out, so why should females be packages of predictability on the racetrack? Here's a system that will help you a lot, whether or not you ascribe to the chauvinist viewpoint.

Watch for a ladies' sprint race where a front-running favorite is carrying 119 pounds or more. Take the mare or filly that has the next-best speed rating in the race, and shows the next-highest odds on the board, and bet one unit on her to win and two units to place.

High weight tends to knock females off stride coming out of the gate. A front-running favorite often gets shuffled back and loses all chance when she's forced to close on the leaders. This is a good spot-bet situation *provided* the favorite has never won carrying as much weight as she's been assigned to carry today.

P.S.: This method also works with male horses, but not as dramatically.

Handicapping Time:
2 minutes at the track

SYSTEM #123
8 POUNDS, 7 POUNDS

Here's a "weighty" tip that's sure to add impact to your picks in races where the horses are three years old and older.

In these races, horses that are getting an 8-pound weight break—whatever the class of race and regardless of distance— deserve special handicapping consideration. For fillies or mares, a 7-pound weight break should earn special attention.

Handicapping Time:

30 minutes reading the program

SYSTEM #124
SUPER WEIGHT

When a super horse goes into competition carrying a crushing weight burden, do not try to guess whether he can pack the mail today. Skip this race!

It's our guess that the racing secretary is trying to get this horse beaten with a pile of stones beneath the saddle. Always be dead sure about the weight factor or your ducats could end up dead in the water.

Handicapping Time:

Only as long as it takes at the track

SYSTEM #125
RAZOR SHARP LINE

You've heard of the long blue line, the thin white line and the Mason-Dixon line, right? Now, here's a razor sharp line to add to your repertoire. It's simple, short, and did I mention *sharp*?

In putting together a razor-fine handicapping line, weight *on* is easier to figure than weight *off*.

Pretty sharp tip, huh?

Handicapping Time:

Only as long as it takes to read the program

SYSTEM #126
WALTER THE WEIGHT WATCHER

W. W. Walter doped this system out while attending Weight Watchers of America at Saratoga. He suggests that you always keep the following tip in mind when using any weight system of handicapping:

Price-seekers in the crowd always exaggerate the importance of weight off, and minimize the impact of weight on. In stabbing for longer-priced winners that are in the race with a feather on top, they create overlays in the betting on the first and second favorites.

Find these overlays and you'll find a delectable dessert waiting for you at the pay window—sugarless, of course!

Handicapping Time:
Only as long as it takes to read the program

SYSTEM #127
CAN'T SEE A WIN

Some horses consistently run near the front alongside another early speed merchant, but refuse to go on and grab the brass ring. They have their counterparts on the greyhound tracks—they're called "pacer" dogs because they always show early speed and chalk up a lot of money finishes, but seldom win.

The problem can be one of eyesight or fear. The animal is just too timid to bolt ahead on its own but will neatly "pace" alongside to get second, third or fourth.

This horse will take your money and spit in your eye! Hence, bet him at your risk. You'll wind up seeing not a whit better than he does.

Handicapping Time:
Only as long as it takes at the track

10 INTERNATIONAL HANDICAPPING SYSTEMS

Sharp punters overseas have developed hard-hitting systems of play. Here's a collection from racing centers around the globe. Book a flight, grab your bags, and you're off to the races in overseas places both exotic and exciting.

SYSTEM #128
WEIGHT ADJUSTMENTS

IRELAND

Weight is a great leveler. The effect of weight can be directly equated to distance. The following table is generally acceptable to students of form.

WEIGHT & DISTANCE			
Length of Course	Difference Produced at Finish Line		
	Half-length	Three Quarters	One Length
5f	1 lb.	2 lb.	3 lb.
6f-10f	1 lb.	1 lb.	2 lb.
11f & over	-	1 lb.	1 lb.

Handicapping Time:
One hour reading the program

SYSTEM #120
FORM-FACT-OPINION

ENGLAND

Form = fact + opinion is a formula the Brits use to perfection. But for form to be of value, the facts must be accurate and the opinions must be expert. Try this method for evaluating them.

In handicapping the next major stakes event, assign a rating of 75 percent to "Known Facts." Give a rating of 25 percent to "Opinion."

This method of evaluation has made English handicappers all the merrier.

Handicapping Time:

Only as long as it takes to read the program

Words to the Wise

Bad systems and lack of planning can dissipate one's capital very rapidly, but sensible methods cut down the loss rate and enable backers to profit more frequently throughout the season. On the course, it should be an axiom of punters to bet and withdraw, if necessary. Plan the campaign before reaching the course, study the card, weigh up trainers' prospects and arrive at a decision for one, two or three bets.

—Winning Racing Guide, London

SYSTEM #130
PROPORTIONATE PROGRESSIVE BETTING

ENGLAND

Active horseplayers in England use an increase of one-quarter, one-half, three-quarters, and a full unit in their basic unit-betting method as a "protected" progressive wagering system. Here's how they do it across the pond:

Start with one betting unit. Make it 2 percent of your total bankroll, for security.

After a loser, increase your bet to two units. Again a loser, increase to three units. More losers: 5, 8, 12, 19 for a total of 50 betting units.

Always return to the minimum after you post a winner, even if it has dead-heated and shows a loss. This allows for "cover" at approximately 6 to 4 at any time, as well as for a losing run of six. If seven successive duds are backed, start over.

Using this plan, when you've gained 25 points (units), you increase your bets in 25 percent increments. And as your profits mount, you hike the action proportionately. Make your bets are to win only. Here's the scale for handy reference:

UNITS INCREASE FOR SERIES OF 17 BETS	
Units Up	Bet Increase
25 units up:	¼ , 2 ½ , 3 ¾ , 6 ¼ , 10, 15, 25
50 units up:	½ , 3, 4 ½ ,7 ½, 12, 18, 30
75 units up:	¾ , 3 ½ ,5 ¾ , 8 ¾ , 14, 21, 35
100 units up:	2, 4, 6, 10, 16, 24, 40
150 units up:	2 ½ , 5, 7 ½ , 12 ½ , 20, 30, 50
200 units up:	3, 6, 9, 15, 24, 36, 60
300 units up:	4, 8, 12, 20, 32, 48, 80
400 units up:	5, 10, 15, 25, 40, 60, 100

Handicapping Time:
Only as long as it takes to read the program

SYSTEM #131
THE GERMAN SYSTEM

GERMANY

Seeking to separate closely matched Teutonic thoroughbreds, horseplayers in Germany follow this maxim:

In races between two evenly-matched horses, the older horse always wins.

It's short, that's for sure, but this German maxim gives Berliners maximum profit.

Handicapping Time:
30 second at the track

SYSTEM #132
WENDY'S WAY

ENGLAND

If it's action you crave, here's a system Wendy welded together just for you. It produces chalk runners, longshots, horses for courses, and good ones just coming to hand. So, stand by for action, clear the decks, and grease the saddles!

Horses selected for this system are placed in groups, and each horse is followed with a level bet until the group as a whole shows a profit. The whole of the group is then discarded.

Selections for groups are chosen at the end of each day's racing, and a group of horses (not less than 6 or more than 30) is then formed. Special note is taken of good winners, seconds, thirds, unlucky horses, and horses that were unexpectedly backed heavily. This is the way that a fresh list of horses is compiled every racing day—and every horse in every group is backed with a level bet each time it runs until the group shows a profit of at least one point. The group is then scrapped.

On the other hand, if 20 bets fail to produce a profit, the group is again scrapped. Backers may choose their own method of forming groups, but the following alpha ratings may be helpful:

ALPHA RATINGS	
"A"	All winners
"B"	All seconds
"C"	All thirds (providing there are eight runners)
"D"	All first and second favorites
"E"	All third-favorites (providing there are eight runners)
"F"	All horses finishing fourth or fifth in large fields and in big races
All horses starting at 10 to 1 or less	

This system calls for a large number of bets to be played daily.

Handicapping Time:
1.5 hours reading the program

SYSTEM #133
A SMASHING (!) SYSTEM

KINGSBURY, BRITAIN

Not all English bettors are all laid-back types. This British bomb is perhaps the wildest system anywhere!

Bet *all* the horses in the first race! You have a winner, whatever the price. Eliminate that horse's post position and, for the next race, bet the next remaining low post to win. Continue through the card.

This system can be used as a longshot method in conjunction with another betting "track" in which you play a more conservative style. Smashing!

Handicapping Time:
Only as long as it takes to read the program

SYSTEM #134
THE 80% SYSTEM

ENGLAND

If you're a smart student of the racing game, this bonus British method offers you a way to study the basic facts and work out a world-beater system. It is based on the fact that first, second and third choices win about 80 percent of all races. We will first give you the system exactly as originally used in England, and then we will offer our comments.

It is an extremely simple play that is easy to finance. The system is devoid of any rules whatsoever—except for price. The progression is so simple that you can read it on the run from a two-decker bus to your flat.

The magic figures are:

ODDS	BET SIZE
2-1	2 bets
3-1	1 bet
4-1	1 bet

Three horses are played for $2, $2, and $2 in any race where the above odds can be obtained. The progression in the 2-to-1 column is two bets. In the 3-to-1 column, it is one bet. And in the 4-to-1 column, the progression also is one. When the 2-to-1 horse wins, you go back one bet; when the 3-to-1 horse wins, you go back two bets; and when the 4-to-1 horse wins, you go back three bets. There is no handicapping!

You simply play the three horses in races that are 2-1, 3-1 and 4-1, or as near to these prices as you can get. For instance, if there is no 2-to-1 horse, take the 5-2 horse. If no horse goes off at 3-1, take 16-5. And if no horse is 4-1, take a horse at 5 to 1. Never go to odds of 6-1. Get the odds within a point or closer if possible.

Analyzing the above system, we find that if the 2-to-1 horse wins the race, you stand to lose only $2 on the entire wager. Apparently, this is an insurance play that will cut down your losses when the first choices are winning. If the 3-to-1 horse wins, you win $2 to the race. And if the 4-to-1 horse wins, you win $4 to the race. At a glance there doesn't seem to be much to this system, but if you figure out the 80 percent of races that horses going off at these prices win the race, it will appear in an entirely different light.

Why not try playing the first three choices in a race? Very often when the favorite does not win, the second or third choices will win—and at exceptionally nice prices. We have not checked out this play yet, so we advise our readers to study it carefully.

"Why play the first choice at all?" you might ask. You bet it for the very good reason that when the first choice wins, it cuts your loss. If you only played the second and third choices every time the favorite won, you would lose two bets. On the other hand, in playing three of them, you are reducing your losses by the amount won on the favorite.

Another line of thought we've come up with is to play the three choices as follows: Bet $6 on the first choice to win, except when he goes to post at even money or less, and bet $8 on him to place. Bet $4 on the second choice to place. And bet $2 on the third choice to show. This progression is based on a different principle than the average method in that you generally are advised to bet more for place and show than to win. The fallacy of this advice lies in the fact that, according to the best opinion and judgment of turf men, the first choice has more chance to win than the third choice has to show. Statistics support this conclusion.

Handicapping Time:
Only as long as it takes to read the program

SYSTEM #135
TOP-WEIGHT SELECTIONS

ENGLAND

Here's a system from the Brits that you can use on any one race at the track. First, choose a race and select the horses as follows:

- List all horses that won their last time out of the gate
- List all horses that won either second or third last time out

Extract from both lists the horses that ran most recently. This gives you the most recent winner and the most recent horse that placed. Choose the horse carrying the most weight in today's race—this horse is the system horse to be backed.

If both horses carry the same weight today, back the two; and of the two horses that won on the same day their last time out, back the one carrying the higher weight. If two of your horses both placed their last time out on the same day, give preference to the second horse over the third horse. If they still tie, again select the one carrying the most weight today.

Handicapping Time:
1.5 hours reading the program

SYSTEM #136
CINCO, SEICO

CARACAS, VENEZUELA

The popular South American 5-6 system has a namesake, adapted for North American handicapping. It's simple but it's dynamite—when you find a horse that qualifies, that is.

Here's the selection process in all its glory: Find a horse that won its last race by five lengths and is back within five days. Or find a horse that won last by six lengths and is back within six days. Parlay? Sure, if you like to live dangerously.

"Is that all there is?" legendary singer Peggy Lee once asked. Yep, that's all, Peg. And often, it's enough!

Handicapping Time:
5 minutes reading the program

SYSTEM #137
PLACING INSURANCE

LIVERPOOL

It was a wise man that suggested that place betting is insurance. If your win bets go down in flames, there is always a chance that the place-bet dividends will cover your stake money.

For any bettor, avoiding losses can be nearly as important as chalking up wins.

Handicapping Time:
Only as long as it takes at the track

SYSTEM #138
THE FRENCH CONNECTION

FRANCE

If you thought the Liverpool play was short 'n sweet, this confection is pure Parisian perfection in its simplicity.

Play the first choice to win and the third choice to show when they are backed down *and* the second choice goes up in the betting.

Handicapping Time:

30 seconds at the track

SYSTEM #139
THE STREAKERS

AUSTRALIA

You don't need to delve deep into the Outback to find the good sense in this nifty tip from Down Under, mates.

"Follow the man in form" is a particularly apt adage that Aussies use when it comes to handicapping jockeys. So often, everything seems to go right for riders who are enjoying a successful run. A string of winners gives most jockeys added confidence. Attempts at difficult tactics and daring maneuvers have a habit of coming off well for those riding on the crest of the wave.

Moreover, the men in form get the best mounts, as owners and trainers tend to refuse jockeys who are not currently riding winners. Jockeys who are out of luck seem to stay out of luck— they lose dash and confidence and often fail to win on horses they should have ridden to the winner's circle.

The bottom line is this: A private account of jockey figures, showing money wins *plus* streak boys, can be among your most highly-priced handicapping tools.

Handicapping Time:

Only as long as it takes at the track

SYSTEM #140
MOVING UP

AUSTRALIA

Here's another tidbit to grill on your handicapping "barbie." This one's a sharp price-play that separates older horses from sophomores in claiming races for 3-year-olds and up.

Pick the 4-year-old with the most weight off that was nearest to second position at any stage of his last race.

This is a great show-play, with quite a number of these picks winning at a long price, maybe even enough to purchase that plane ticket to Sydney.

Handicapping Time:

5 minutes reading the program

SYSTEM #141
ON THE IMPROVE

JAPAN

Anybody from Tokyo that's worth a yen uses this method to find horses "on the improve." Play the horse that has never run less than fourth in his most recent three successive outings *and* has not won in his last six races.

This horse may be an exceptionally fine pick if he has shown an upcurve from fourth to third in his finish positions. Ah, so that's how it goes!

Handicapping Time:

One minute reading the program

SYSTEM #142
PACE DOWN UNDER

NEW ZEALAND

You can't pull the wool over any New Zealand handicapper's eyes—know that Australian jockeys are supreme as judges of pace. They are accustomed to running home gallops with a stopwatch timing every furlong. The best of them are brilliant at delivering their challenge right on the line. In fact, an unreliable horse or a green 2-year-old may scarcely realize he has had a race!

Add points to any fast-closing handicap horse that draws an Australian rider in events with much early speed.

Handicapping Time:
Only as long as it takes at the track

SYSTEM #143
IMPROVEMENT BY WEIGHT

LIVERPOOL

Here's a carefully researched chart of the monthly improvement that should be expected of 3-year-olds at various distances. The chart begins with the first March in which they run, under which you'll find varying race lengths, and continues to the next March.

MONTHLY IMPROVEMENT									
March	April	May	June	July	Aug	Sept	Oct	Next March	12 Month Total
5f 4	2	2	2	3	1	-		1	15
6f 2	3	2	2	2	2	1		4	18
8f 4	3	5	2	2	1	1		6	24
1.5m 3	3	3	3	3	2	2		7	26
2m 2	4	3	4	2	2	-		13	30

All figures represent pounds.

Handicapping Time:
Only as long as it takes to read the program

SYSTEM #144
BUG BOY SPOT

CANADA

Sharp Canadian bettors know that the weight allowance given to apprentice jockeys can give a talented youngster the edge over full-fledged jockeys, provided the horse he's riding is the type of animal that will run kindly for him. In fact, the apprentice sometimes has little more to do than sit in the saddle!

If he succeeds in riding his mount to its best advantage, the weight allowance can prove a decisive race-winning factor. And that's the way that handicappers from Calgary to Toronto bet it.

Handicapping Time:
Only as long as it takes to read the program

SYSTEM #145
J. O. E.

ENGLAND

J.O.E. is our acronym for this system from jolly old England. Take the selections of three leading handicappers for the first and last races on the card. Back them in separate series—that is, the transaction on the first race will be independent of the transaction on the last race and each handicapper's selection is backed independently of the other.

Each losing series will consist of three bets in the proportion of 2-3-5 so that a winner at even money would, at the third bet, recover previous losses in that series. After three losses, no further bet is made on that handicapper's selection for that race until a winner is given, at which time the process is repeated.

Handicapping Time:
55 minutes reading the program

SYSTEM #146
TRUE MARK

NEWMARKET

We've quoted this one almost verbatim from an old British Turf publication. When a horse wins or is narrowly beaten, the track handicapper must decide whether he has improved, or whether the rest of the field has simply run below form. In most cases, the latter will be found to be true.

However, the track handicapper must take the *literal* view. Therefore, he will raise the horse above its true rating.

It will be up to you to scrutinize all handicaps, noting all horses on their true marks, and checking these for signs of a return to form. With experience you will learn to spot these quickly and may have some nice-priced winners as a result.

Handicapping Time:
Only as long as it takes to read the program

SYSTEM #147
IMPROVING CONTENDERS

FRANCE

This is a Parisian system that has been wonderfully successful at the pari-mutuels in France and has produced winning tickets of very large sums of money. The object is to select a horse that has won, and then has lost within 20 days of winning his last outing. In other words, the steed has suffered a complete form reversal.

Preference is always given in selection to horses that run very far back in the losing race. No horse should be selected unless he has won a race in better than the following times:

FORM REVERSAL		
	Fast Track	Heavy Track
6 furlongs	1:12	1:15
1 mile	1:38	1:42
1.70 mile	1:44	1:46
1 1/16 mile	1:45	1:48
1 1/8 mile	1:51	1:56

Adjust these times to an effective variant for the track you play.

Here's an example of how the system works:

Golden Billows won on May 28th. In his next out on June 12th, he lost by 16 lengths. Play started on his next race with a wager of $5. Again Golden Billows lost, finishing second. In the next race, $10 was played, but GB was beaten again, this time by 12 lengths. On his third start, the bet increased to $15. Golden Billows won and paid $77.25 to the $15 wager.

And *oui*, you'll need patience and some capital for this progression play, but if you're successful at it, it may turn out to be golden.

Handicapping Time:

55 minutes reading the program

SYSTEM #148
PATIENT LONGSHOT

GERMANY

Some bright young man from Mannheim came up with this system for picking longshot winners. Find a good horse that has posted a good third place or second place. However, he then runs *below* these figures, and then shows a *flash*.

If you play such horses, you will post some winners. Of course, you will need to be patient. And a follow-up play is nearly always essential.

Handicapping Time:
  2 minutes at the track

SYSTEM #149
THE BEATEN CHOICE

ENGLAND

  Blokes from Britain like this beaten-favorites method that is based on a progression of bets. When a favorite finishes second, it becomes a system horse. This system calls for backing this beaten favorite until it wins, but not more than three times. The stakes increase according to these guidelines:

  The first bet is $2. The second bet is $4. The third bet is $6, and so on.

  If two or more system horses are engaged in the same race, back only the horse that started at the longest price when first coming into the system. But if both horses started at the same price, back the one finishing nearest the winner.

  When a horse wins, he is struck off the system. After two months of entering the system, horses should be struck off even though they have not run three times. Horses may re-qualify at a later date if they meet the system's requirements.

Handicapping Time:
  30 minutes reading the program

SYSTEM #150
WEIGHT & TIME

ENGLAND

It is difficult to relate weight carried with a horse's expected racing performance. However, this clever charting system offers some genuine help. A class handicapper in Great Britain worked this one out.

A good general indicator for relating pounds to fractions of a second is to equate 15 pounds with a second. In other words, 15 pounds = 1 full second.

Note that in practice, these figures will prove more realistic for sprint races up to 1 mile. This equation, however, can be used for all distances by adjusting the weight impact upward.

Handicapping Time:

Only as long as it takes at the track

Words From the Wise

"How important are speed-pace-class-distance-track condition-weight-jockey-and-trainer? What role do they play in determining the outcome of a race? Are there patterns of predictability? Is the game based on logic or ruled by chance? And at rock bottom, is it possible to play the game well enough to overcome the stiff 20 per cent betting tax and still show a profit for the effort? The clues are complex, sometimes contradictory. The secrets of the game are subtle and elusive. And there is so much bad advice floating around."

—Steven Davidowitz

ATTENTION: HORSE PLAYERS!

If you like this book, come to our website, and browse our extensive library of titles—we not only have the world's largest selection of horse titles (*more than 25 times* the selection of major chain superstores), but over 3,000 total gaming and gambling titles!